EDGE
BOOKS™

ALL
ABOUT
Dogs

GREAT DANES

by Tammy Gagne

Consultant: Lourdes Carvajal
Vice President, Great Dane Club of America
Judge, American Kennel Club

Capstone
press®

Mankato, Minnesota

Edge Books are published by Capstone Press,
151 Good Counsel Drive, P.O. Box 669, Mankato, Minnesota 56002.
www.capstonepress.com

Library of Congress Cataloging-in-Publication Data
Gagne, Tammy.
    Great Danes / by Tammy Gagne.
    p. cm. — (Edge books. All about dogs)
    Includes bibliographical references and index.
    Summary: "Describes the history, physical features, temperament, and
care of the Great Dane breed" — Provided by publisher.
    ISBN-13: 978-1-4296-2301-8 (hardcover)
    ISBN-10: 1-4296-2301-2 (hardcover)
    1. Great Dane — Juvenile literature. I. Title. II. Series.
SF429.G7G27 2009
636.73 — dc22   2008026936

Editorial Credits
Jennifer Besel, editor; Veronica Bianchini, designer; Marcie Spence,
    photo researcher

Photo Credits: All photos by Capstone Press/Karon Dubke except:
Alamy/blickwinkel/Schlotterbeck, 5; The London Art Archive, 11
Courtesy of Norvel Benoit at I've Spotted Great Danes, 14
Getty Images Inc./Brooke/Topical Press Agency, 15
Mary Evans Picture Library, 13
Peter Arnold/Biosphoto/Labat Jean-Michel, 7
Sandy Schneider, 22
Shutterstock/Rick's Photography, 9

1 2 3 4 5 6 14 13 12 11 10 09

Table of Contents

CHAPTER 1

LOYAL AND BRAVE

A Great Dane runs alongside its owner, the look of a smile across its face. There's nothing this dog loves more than its owner. And for the owner, there is no better dog friend in the world.

Great Danes are best known for their large size. These dogs stand head and shoulders above most other breeds. Some people say a Great Dane looks more like a small horse than a dog. But even though they are large, Great Danes are not frightful animals. These dogs' friendly and faithful personalities are even bigger than their size.

Great Danes are loyal,
fun-loving dogs.

Part of the Family

Great Danes are very loyal and brave. They form strong bonds with their human family members. They make excellent guard dogs for this reason. But Great Danes are not mean-spirited. These giant dogs make surprisingly gentle pets.

Great Danes enjoy attention, but owners must be watchful. Because of their large size, playful Great Danes can accidently knock over small children.

Great Danes form bonds with their families and will protect them if necessary.

Great Dane puppies are very active. Big backyards and regular walks are ideal for them. These energetic puppies can grow into lazy adults, though. Adult Great Danes will nap on the furniture all day if you let them. A walk is a good way to exercise your Great Dane. Letting it play in a fenced yard is also a great way to make sure it gets exercise.

EDGE FACT

Great Danes usually have eight to 10 puppies in a litter.

On its hind legs, an adult Great Dane is taller than its owner.

Is This Dog for You?

Many people buy Great Dane puppies before fully understanding the dogs' needs or how big they will grow. Many Great Danes have been given up to animal shelters and rescue organizations by people who couldn't care for these large dogs. If you think this breed may be right for you, consider adopting an adult dog in need of a new home.

You'll need to find a good **breeder** if you want a Great Dane puppy. Breeders registered by the American Kennel Club (AKC) will have healthy, well-cared-for puppies. Whether you get a puppy or adopt an adult, you'll want to learn all you can about the breed. With good information, you can be a great dog owner.

breeder — someone who breeds and raises dogs

CHAPTER 2

GREAT DANE HISTORY

Over the years, the Great Dane has gone by many names, like wolf dog, German mastiff, or English dogge. No one is quite sure why the breed came to be called the Great Dane. From the name, you would think that this dog was developed in Denmark. However, that's not the case. The Great Dane breed began in Germany about 400 years ago. Historians believe the Irish wolfhound, the greyhound, and the Old English mastiff were bred together. German breeders wanted to create a strong, quick dog that could be used for hunting. The result was the Great Dane.

Hunting Wild Boar

In Germany, the Great Dane was used mainly to hunt wild boar. This hoglike creature was fast and mean. The dog that hunted it had to be swift and athletic. The Great Dane was perfect for the job.

Hunting wild boar was a dangerous and painful job for early Great Danes.

EDGE FACT

Great Danes have gone by many names. In Germany, the breed is still known as *Deutsche dogge*, or German mastiff.

Hunting wild boar was a terrible job. The dogs battled with the vicious boars. Often the boars' tusks would rip off all or part of a dog's ear. As a result, breeders began **cropping** Great Danes' ears. Breeders would cut away the outer parts of the puppies' ears. The cropped ears stood straight up, instead of flopping to the side.

cropped ear

normal ear

EDGE FACT

Great Danes are rarely used for hunting today. But some owners still have their puppies' ears cropped. An anesthetic is used, though, so the process isn't painful for the dogs.

crop — to cut away the outer parts of a dog's ear

Great Danes in America

In the late 1800s, German owners began showing their Great Danes in national dog shows. The breed was also becoming more and more popular around the world. An American named Francis Butler first brought Great Danes to the United States in 1857. The breed is still well liked in the United States today, but it is not the most popular. In 2007, the Great Dane was ranked number 23 among the American Kennel Club's most registered breeds.

Dog shows made the Great Dane a popular breed in Germany.

Almost Lost in the War

World War I (1914–1918) was an especially difficult time for the Great Dane breed. During the war, people all over Europe struggled to find enough food to survive. Food for dogs was even harder to come by. Many Great Danes died of **starvation**, and breeding almost completely stopped. The breed was close to extinction. After the war, breeders were determined to bring the Great Dane back. They had trouble finding enough dogs to continue the breed. But slowly, breeders rebuilt the population of Great Danes.

During World War I, a few military officers kept Great Danes.

starvation — suffering from a lack of food

In the 1920s, Great Danes
were back on the rise.

CHAPTER 3

STRONG AND PROUD

Great Danes project an image of strength. Nearly every part of this dog's body is muscular. What makes the breed stand out, though, is its balanced appearance. Great Danes may be big, but they never look clumsy.

Great Danes are among the largest dog breeds. A male Great Dane stands about 35 inches (89 centimeters) tall at its shoulders. Females are usually a couple of inches shorter. Larger Great Danes are favored in dog shows. Males less than 30 inches (76 centimeters) and females less than 28 inches (71 centimeters) aren't even allowed in the ring.

Dogs this big are not lightweight. Females weigh 100 to 130 pounds (45 to 59 kilograms). Males weigh up to 200 pounds (91 kilograms).

Great Danes stand strong and balanced.

Great Danes' coats can be different colors. Six colors are considered acceptable in the show ring. Fawn dogs have a gold coat and a black face. Brindle dogs have a gold coat with black stripes over their bodies. Dogs that are black and white are called either harlequin or mantle. A mantle dog's body is white with a black blanket of color across its back. Harlequin dogs have patches of black all over their white bodies. Great Danes may also be solid black or a steel color called blue.

A Great Dane's eyes truly show its personality. Its eyes are dark and of medium size. The look in the eyes shows a proud, intelligent expression. The eyes should never look mean.

a blue Great Dane

a brindle Great Dane

Merle-colored dogs, like this one, are not allowed in the show ring, but they still make good pets.

EDGE FACT

A Great Dane looks tough, but its short coat offers little protection from the cold. Many owners use dog coats to keep their Great Danes warm on winter walks.

Regular walks help keep a Great Dane happy and healthy.

Temperament

Great Danes have big personalities. These dogs are friendly, loyal, and eager to please their owners. A courageous spirit makes these dogs very protective of their human families. But if nothing is going on, they enjoy a long nap too.

Great Danes make good house pets for the right people. They are very active, but they don't need as much space as you might imagine. If trained properly, Great Danes can be surprisingly calm at home. They can even live in apartments, as long as owners take them outside for exercise regularly.

Gentle Giants

Great Danes are very intelligent. They can often tell when people are sad or upset. Their big hearts make them good at comforting sick or injured people. With training, Great Danes can work as therapy dogs. Therapy dogs learn to be calm even if their tails are pulled or their eyes are poked. They also learn not to be afraid of loud noises, wheelchairs, or screaming. Once the dogs are trained and licensed, owners can take them to hospitals or disaster sites to help support those who need it.

Great Danes are used as therapy dogs for the elderly.

EDGE FACT

Therapy dogs, including Great Danes, helped people after the attacks on September 11, 2001. The dogs comforted rescue workers and families. The dogs' wagging tails and wet kisses put smiles on many people's faces.

23

CHAPTER 4

CARING FOR A GREAT DANE

Caring for a Great Dane is a big job in many ways. These large dogs must be trained early, fed properly, and groomed regularly. Great Danes need plenty of exercise. They also need lots of attention and affection. Caring for a dog of this size is a big commitment.

Training a Great Dane

An adult Great Dane will often weigh as much as its owner. Size alone makes early training a must. Great Danes must be taught simple commands as early as possible. These commands include "sit," "lie down," and "stay." The dogs also need be **socialized**. They need to meet many people so they aren't afraid of strangers.

socialize — to train to get along with people and other dogs

Great Danes love attention from their owners.

A responsible Great Dane breeder begins training puppies before they go home with their new families. But owners must continue training their dogs at home. No dog will learn everything in a single day. Work on one command at a time until the dog knows it. Then begin working on another.

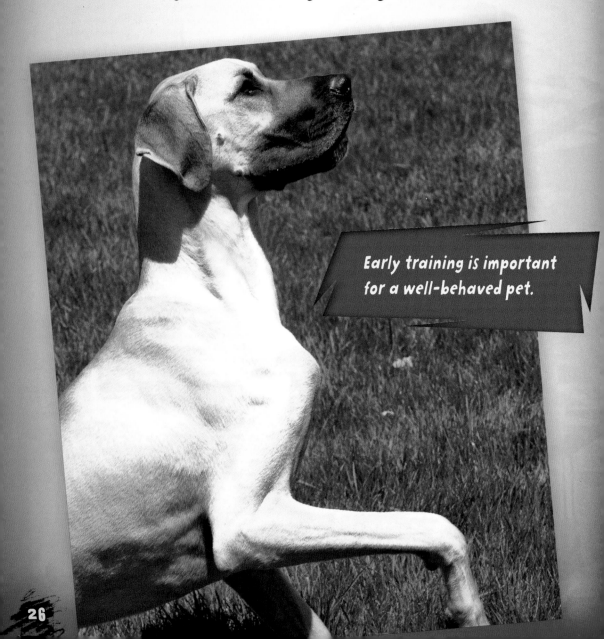

Early training is important for a well-behaved pet.

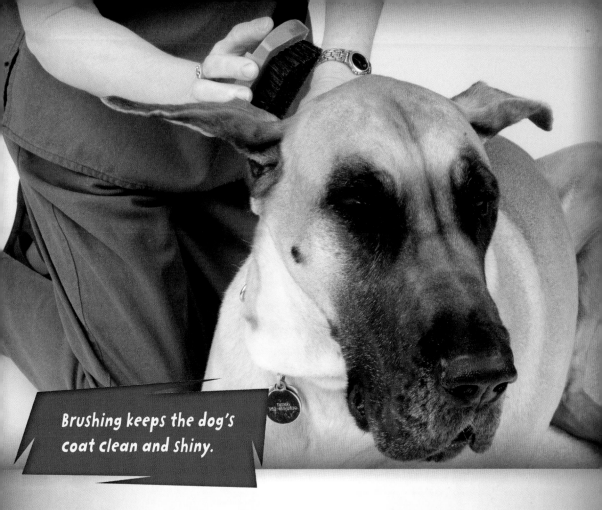

Brushing keeps the dog's coat clean and shiny.

Daily Care

Keeping your Great Dane healthy begins with proper feeding and grooming. Feed your Great Dane a high-quality dog food twice a day. It is tempting to let a dog this big eat as much as it wants, but don't. Overweight dogs face a greater risk of health issues, such as heart disease and joint problems.

A Great Dane's short hair needs to be brushed about once a week. The dog also needs its nails clipped regularly. If you can hear your dog's nails scrape the floor when it walks, your Great Dane is overdue for a trim.

Vet Trips

One of the best ways to keep your dog feeling its best is regular visits to a veterinarian. The vet will examine your Great Dane's body, listen to its heart, and give it any necessary **vaccinations**. The vet will also check your Great Dane's hips. This breed often has joint problems.

During your dog's first exam, talk to your vet about having your dog spayed or neutered. This simple operation prevents an animal from having offspring and helps control the pet population.

Also talk to your vet about bloat. Bloat is a condition where the stomach fills with gas and then twists over. Large breeds are more at risk for bloat than smaller dogs. Bloat can cause death in Great Danes if not found in time. Talk to your vet about ways to prevent bloat.

You can help your dog live a full and healthy life by staying on top of all its needs. Each time you trim your dog's nails or take it to the vet, you are showing how much you love it. A Great Dane will love you back like it does everything else — in a big way.

vaccination — medicine that protects animals from disease

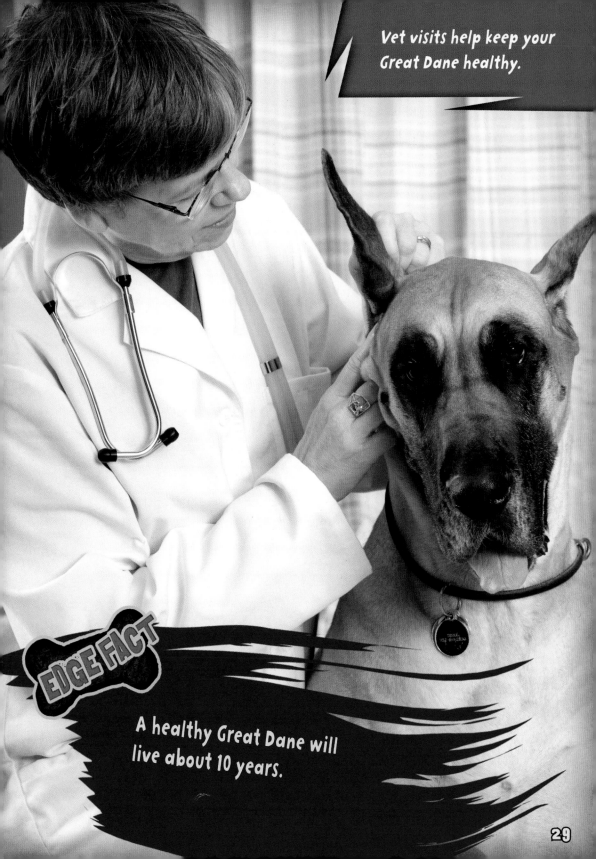

Vet visits help keep your Great Dane healthy.

EDGE FACT

A healthy Great Dane will live about 10 years.

29

Glossary

anesthetic (an-iss-THET-ik) — a drug that makes animals sleep so doctors can perform surgery on them

breed (BREED) — a certain kind of animal within an animal group; breed also means to mate and raise a certain kind of dog.

breeder (BREE-duhr) — someone who breeds and raises dogs or other animals

crop (KROP) — to cut away the outer parts of a dog's ear

neuter (NOO-tur) — to operate on a male animal so it is unable to produce young

socialize (SOH-shuh-lize) — to train to get along with people and other dogs

spay (SPAY) — to operate on a female animal so it is unable to produce young

starvation (star-VAY-shuhn) — the condition of suffering or dying from lack of food

vaccination (vak-suh-NAY-shun) — a shot of medicine that protects animals from a disease

Read More

Fiedler, Julie. *Great Danes*. Tough Dogs. New York: PowerKids Press, 2006.

Murray, Julie. *Great Danes*. Dogs. Edina, Minn.: Abdo, 2003.

Tagliaferro, Linda. *Therapy Dogs*. Dog Heroes. New York: Bearport, 2005.

Internet Sites

FactHound offers a safe, fun way to find educator-approved Internet sites related to this book.

Here's what you do:

1. Visit *www.facthound.com*
2. Choose your grade level.
3. Begin your search.

This book's ID number is 9781429623018.

FactHound will fetch the best sites for you!

Index